True Treasure Stories From Key West to Amelia Island

MARITIME ARCHAEOLOGIST
SCOTT R. JENSEN M.A.

authorHOUSE

AuthorHouse™
1663 Liberty Drive
Bloomington, IN 47403
www.authorhouse.com
Phone: 833-262-8899

Published by AuthorHouse 09/14/2023

ISBN: 979-8-8230-1292-8 (sc)
ISBN: 979-8-8230-1291-1 (e)

Library of Congress Control Number: 2023915447

Print information available on the last page.

Any people depicted in stock imagery provided by Getty Images are models, and such images are being used for illustrative purposes only. Certain stock imagery © Getty Images.

This book is printed on acid-free paper.

DEDICATION

Sometimes we forget the people we care about the most; my family and all of my friends. This book will be my last I will write. I have enjoyed writing the trilogy about Amelia Island, it's a been pleasure.

Thanks for everyone's contributions.

CONTENTS

CONTENTS

INTRODUCTION

This publication takes the reader thru my eyes, it describes actual events that I have witnessed and taken part of. It starts in Key West Florida and continues up the coast to Amelia Island. During my excavations I have found airplanes, concrete trucks, bombs, land mines and of course treasure!

☩ CHAPTER ONE ☩

Pirates of the Marquesas

I<small>T WAS A COLD AND</small> rainy day as I approached the Jacksonville International Airport in Florida. I picked up a rental car and headed for Key West. When you get to the first Key it is the slow going, the speed limit is 35 or lower.

It took me around 8 hours to get to Key West, and I was really tired. The sun was just going down when I turned my car to the Key West Airport. I took a cab to the docks and located the research vessel. The sun was going down and this was what I saw............

Figure 1   A Key Deer at night

Figure 1.2   Key West at sunrise

The crew were expecting me when I located the research vessel. I was tired and went to my bunk and quickly feel asleep. I slept like a baby. Before the sun came up, I heard the motors crank up, this was the divers alarm clock.

This was strange to me as it was one hour before sunrise. We had a new Captain and I thought it was something new in his procedure. I looked out of the window as the crane was loading a tarp covered item roughly 20 feet in length. We were told to go back to our bunks and sleep in as we were going out the following day.

My crewmates and I went to too walk Key West most Southern Point Buoy, that was Mile Marker 1. However, we had another 36 miles in the research vessel, by water to get to the *Santa Margarita / Nuestra Senora de Atocha* site.

These sites were found by famed treasure hunter Mel Fisher in 1980 and 1985 and they are still looking. This was the treasure of 1622 and it contained a massive amount of treasure!

When the research vessel left the Port of Key West, we headed towards the "Lakes" a patch of calm water. After the "Lakes" (11.6 nautical miles out) it was very rough, we were going to where the Atlantic Ocean turned into the Gulf of Mexico. This was our destination when the weather was bad; it was sunny on the Marquesas Key. (6.2 nautical miles).

I found it strange that we stopped. The Captain said there was bad weather and we were remaining here for a few days. The crew got our fishing poles out, and fished until the next morning. We headed to our bunks. It was surprising to me that in the morning the crane on the research vessel was running.

I looked out of the window and saw a Louisiana mud boat hanging from the cable on the crane. I thought "wow" this is not normal. As the boat was put in the water, three people got in and sped away. They were headed to the Marquesas Key.

This Key was illegal to trespass on. This posed a problem in my mind. What should I do?

Figure 2   Marquesas Key from the air

After I consulted the crew, we decide to turn them in. However, there was a problem, the phones had no signal. They were all digital phones. Digital need several phone towers to relay the signal and none were available.

That being said, I had an analog phone. Analog phones were being phased-out but the signal could reach Key West. The research vessel had three levels, if I stood on the roof of the third level, I could get a signal!

I turned them in. I called the National Oceanic and Atmospheric Administration (NOAA). NOAA flew a plane with infrared imaging and recorded them at the back the of the island.

After a few hours an 80-foot law enforcement ship pulled anchored about 60 feet from the research vessel. The ship contained men and women standing on the deck with M-16's. They took a skiff over to our vessel and said "your vessel belongs to us". We assured them that we were the ones that called them.

The Vice President member called the President of the research vessel in Fernandina Beach Florida and he and a friend were on their way. Fernandina Beach to Key West is a long way, when they arrive at the island, that had to get a vessel and go to the Marquesas Key.

Meanwhile, the Law Enforcement Officers took the crews ID and went back to vessel and waited for the pirates to come back. At dusk, the pirates came back to the research vessel. As they came back in the Louisiana Mud boat, we pulled them up with the crane onto the deck. They had a big surprise when they saw Officers with M-16's on the deck.

It was the newly hired Captain and two other people in the mud boat.

The Law Enforcement Officers asked them what they were doing behind the Marquesas Key. The Captain said we were just touring. Wow! They searched the mud boat and found a six-shooter (weapon) and an underwater metal detector.

The took the ID's of the Captain and his cohorts and waited for the President of the research vessel to arrive. The President arrived the next day and he fired them all.

The pirates used a Louisiana Mud boat because of the small amount of water it took to float the boat. There were rumors that when the Spanish were salvaging the *Santa Margarita* in 1622 that some of the Spanish soldiers buried some of the treasure on the back side of the Marquises Key. These Spanish solders where supposedly executed.

The fired Captain was by told the Law Enforcement Agents to take them to the spot that they had excavated. Wow! The pirates had a boardwalk, money bags, a pump and a dug a gigantic deep hole.

They were told to excavated at the site by a guy who had satellite access out in California, and he had found a depression on the back side if the island. I remember the pirates telling us that if they dug the hole three feet deeper, we would have been rich!

NOAA asked the President of the research vessel to dig the site up as they wanted to put this myth to rest; he refused on basis of destruction of the environment. I agreed about the environmental factors, that being said, it would have been awesome!

They asked the Law Enforcement Agency, they replied "we don't do mud", the Coast Guard refused and that was that............ I wanted to complete the mission as the damage was done, but the President of research vessel was adamant. So, I bowed to his wishes.

The President of the research vessel hired another Captain and we went to the *Santa Margarita* site. This is some of the samples of what we found.............................

Figure 3   The author at the site

Figure 4   Metal Detecting

The research vessel contains an Excavator which is powered by a hydraulic pump. This powers a crane that lifts the Excavator off the deck and into the ocean. It has the capacity to excavates a 60-foot hole in width and a 35-foot depth.

That is an impressive hole!

Figure 5   Treasure Excavator

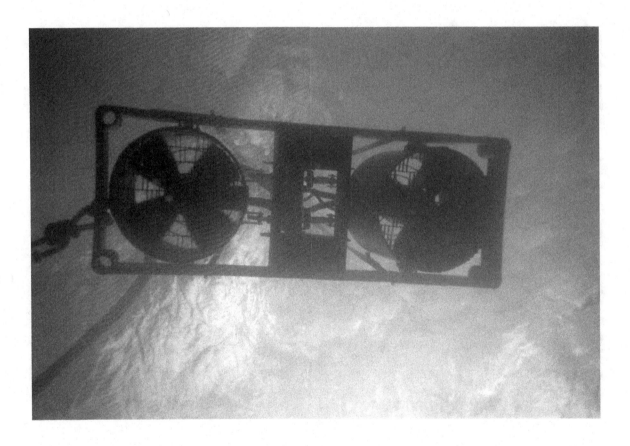

Figure 6   Just hanging around the Excavator 0 0

Figure 7 Metal Detector and Mask

These are the tools of the trade for a Maritime Archaeologist. It allows me to go down into an excavated hole to find clues to artifacts or even treasure!

Figure 8   Diving for Treasure

Figure 9   Nuggets and a Filigree Bead

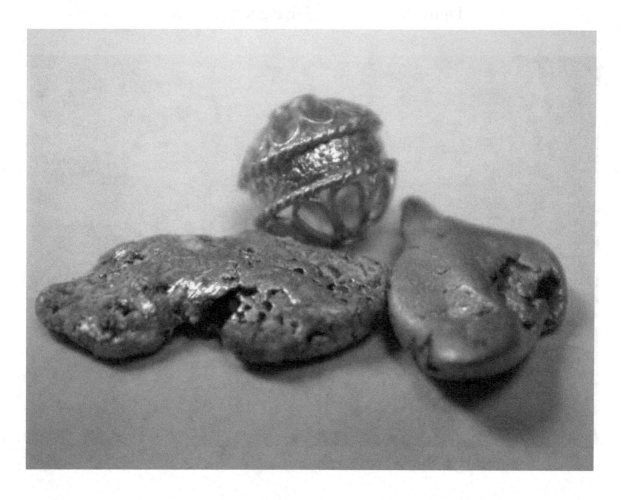

Figure 10   Gold Flakes

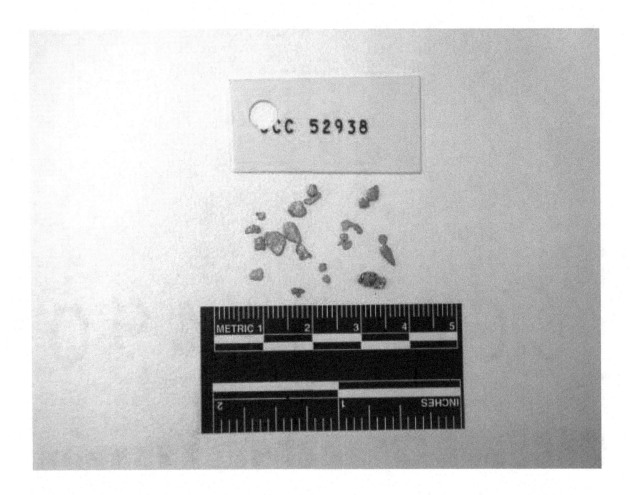

Figure 11   Treasure Nuggets 1

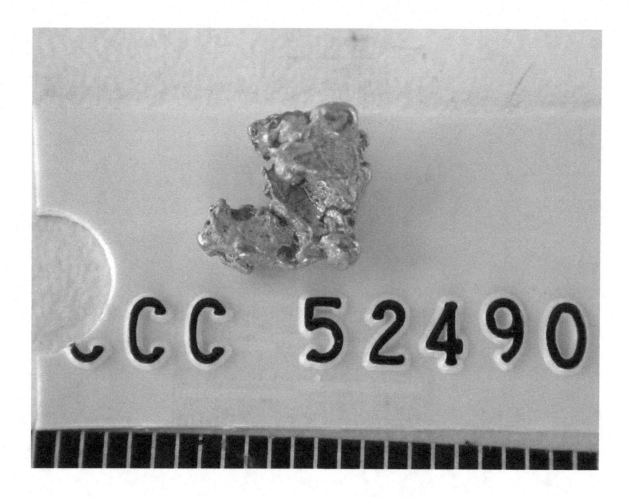

Figure 12   Treasure Nuggets 2

Figure 13   Ring and Nuggets

Figure 14   Captain EO and the first Gold

On Figure 14 it was gold, however, nothing is as it seems. It was part of a bomb; the trigger was made of gold because the salt water would not corrode it!

What was the bomb doing at the bottom of the ocean? Turns out bombs were everywhere along the Florida coastline. They practiced for D-Day in WWII. I have found bombs, missiles, land mines and everything in between! Some of them were inert and some them were live!

When diving be responsible, don't bring anything on your vessel that is that is unexploded!!!!

⊰ CHAPTER TWO ⊱

Emerald in a Conch Shell

On September 11th 2002 I was diving like I do every day. I was on the *Santa Margarita* site and it was a beautiful day. When I entered the water, something that piqued my interest.

It was a conch shell; the biggest one I have ever seen. I was an educator and part time diver and was collecting shells for a classroom display. Of course, my main focus was treasure on the *Margarita* site, but I had to place it on the deck of the research vessel.

I dove about twelve weeks and I gathered my shells up in a waterproof bag and took them to my classroom. When the students got finished with their assignment early, I would let them clean the shells in my lab (I taught science). I just wanted sand out of the out of the shells.

A student rushed out of the lab and said he had a green rock packed in the sand. I recognize it immediately as an emerald. Not only was it big, it was huge!

I called Fernandina Beach Florida were our dive shop was located and told them what I had found.

A friend at a jeweler shop put the emerald on the scale and it weighed in at 40.2 carats. Wow! That was one big emerald...

Figure 15   Emerald

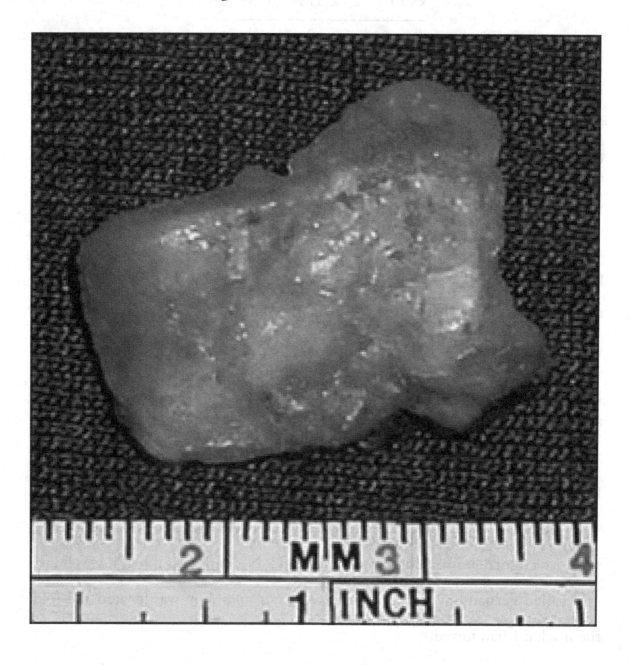

I surmised that the conch shell had many emeralds in it and someone boarded the *Santa Margarita* and told them it was the biggest shell they had ever seen! This souvenir was packed with sand, whose purpose was to get it on the vessel to smuggle these precious stones! If an individual was caught smuggling, they would be put to death!

Figure 16   Conch Shell

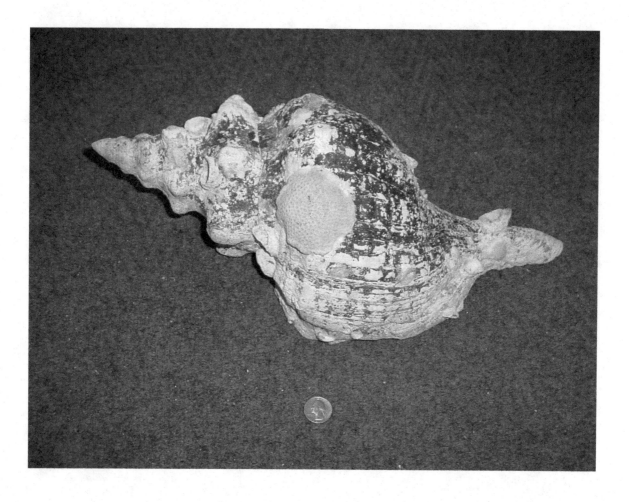

Some other pictures of the massive emerald that I had discovered on the *Margarita* site.

Figure 17   A gentleman holding the Emerald

Figure 18   Emerald in a conch shell in comparison to a United State Quarter

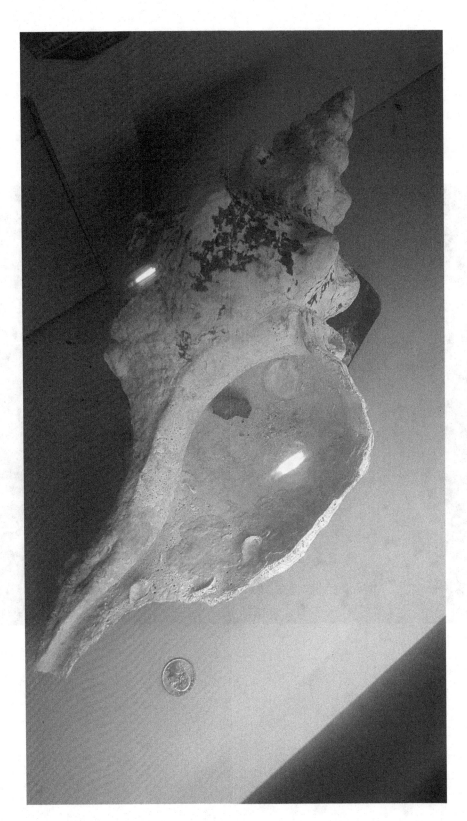

Figure 19   Conch Shell 1

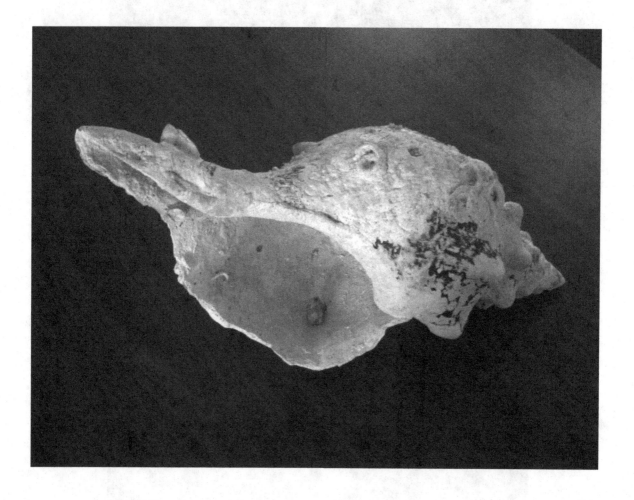

Figure 20   Conch Shell 2

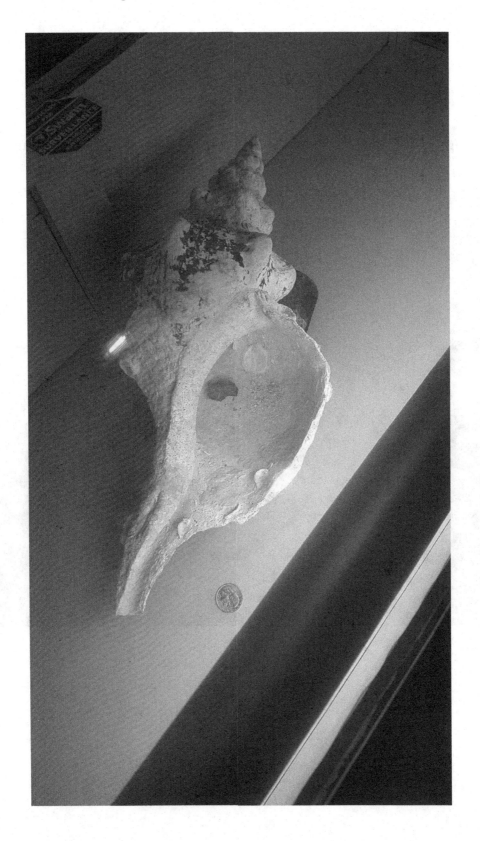

Figure 21   Summer storm that created a Waterspout

Figure 22   Waterspout

Figure 23 Waterspout 2

Figure 23.2 Emerald Find

❧ CHAPTER THREE ❧

Jupiter Inlet

JUPITER INLET IS HOME TO the *San Miguel Archangel* which sank in 1659, a massive amount of rare coins was found on this shipwreck. As the story goes, a hurricane had just hit the park and washed a good amount of the coast away. The next day a lifeguard was swimming laps over the washed-out area and saw cannons.

(Two surfers actually spotted them the day before).

In 1987, the lifeguard and a marina owner formed a joint venture, filed a Federal Admiralty Claim and it was approved. Soon, in the same year, the Federal admiralty court deeded all the ships in Florida to the State. It was called the "Abandoned Shipwreck Act". That means that the Jupiter wreck site would work under the rules of the State of Florida. (And sometimes the Federal Court).

Figure 23.4 Sunset at Jupiter

Jupiter is a place of mystery, it has gold and silver, and everything in- between. The water is clear and you can actually see! I am a black water diver, when the research vessel goes down south it is a pleasure to find treasure!

I found a ballast stone with my underwater metal detector. You can pick up a ballast stone because of it mineral content, which many have. This one was special!

Figure 24   Ballast Stone

So, what are ballast stones? Ballast stones were used to keep the ship level, they lined up along the keel (the keel runs down the center of the vessel) to keep the ship from rolling over and sinking.

Ballast stones are all shape and sizes. The ship always had stones in the hull, it was how many! When a treasure ship (or any ship) was loaded, there was not the amount ballast stones as if it were empty.

The *San Miguel Archangel* was not empty, it was fully loaded with rare silver coins, gold coins, and much more. The funny thing was a lack of cultural items; very little pottery, spoons, and pots.

The following photographs are of the artifact cleaning table and the cleaning process on the table.

Figure 25   Archaeologist Table with the author.

Figure 26   Working on Ballast Stone

Figure 27   Close up of Ballast Stone

Figure 28   Exposed Treasure Ballast

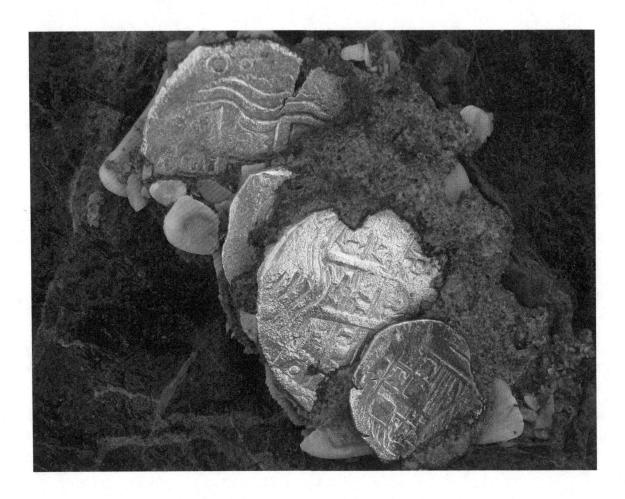

Figure 29   Coins on Ballast Stone

Figure 30   The author holds the ballast with coins

Figure 31   Ballast coins in an aquarium

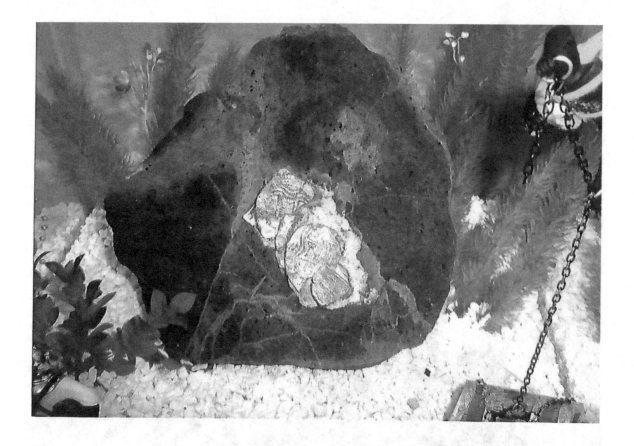

I had a problem, if the ballast stone were removed from the water, over time the stone would crumble. Not all ballast stones would crumble but the I one found was very magnetic, which is a big sign that it would.

I solved the problem! Instead of having four coins and

a crumbling stone, I put it into an aquarium!

Figure 31.1 Treasure!

⚜ CHAPTER FOUR ⚜

Sebastian & 1715 Plate Fleet

THERE IS A CITY IN Florida called Sebastian and the ships were loaded with Spanish Treasure! This area was known as "The Treasure Coast", as ships were scattered along the coastline.

In the 1960's, it is said that people skimmed flat rocks across the ocean only to find out later that they were coins! Since the 1960's until the present, people and groups of people still on search the dunes and on the ocean floor. The 1715 Plate Fleet, some hit the rocks, some foundered, but they all sank! (Four are unaccounted for).

This publication is not meant to be the history of "The Treasure Coast", it is a brief overview of my experiences. (Not all my experiences!).

<u>Sharks!</u>

It was a hot day and the waves were too rough to move the research vessel, so the divers came up with an idea. We were miles away from Sebastian and a diver wanted to dive on what he thought was a shipwreck!

It was the plan that the skiff (boat) would be used to transport the divers to

Sebastian. That was not my plan; I drove my little red truck! I drove the several miles to Sebastian as I was not going through those rough waves. The skiff picked me up and we were on way!

The driver of the skiff had previously recorded the Lat / Long on the Global Positioning Satellite (GPS). He found the spot and anchored the boat. I started to gear up to take the plunge into the sea.

I went roughly 50 feet down to the bottom. What did I find you say? Sand and more sand, however that being said, I found the thing I was looking for. It was the supposed shipwreck.

While I was exploring the supposed shipwreck, something hit me on my facemask. It was a shark! When I got my facemask readjusted, the shark was the going for a second run at my face. I punched **him** in the face!

I don't know what kind of shark it was; Bull, Tiger, Nurse or even Great White shark. They all bite! I looked towards the surface and the skiff was nowhere to be seen.

Believe or not the boat was ½ miles from where I was searching. He was feeding the sharks. Wow, when the sandwich and crackers ran out, the boat had a feeding frenzy around it.

When the was skiff was overhead, there were about 12 to 14 sharks around the it. While the other diver was getting in the in the boat, I hugged a rope hanging off the skiff. There were sharks chewing on my fins, hitting on my legs and jumping out of the water.

The driver of the skiff said he was moving the boat away so the sharks would eat his lunch. I guess he did not a big enough lunch. This was the first time I involved have seen a shark feeding frenzy, and I it will be hopefully the last!

Cabin Wreck

The names of the 1715 Plate Fleet were named after an object that was associated the wreck. This wreck was named the Cabin Wreck. Why? Because this cabin was used by the *Real Eight Company* in the 1960's to live and stockpile treasure and artifacts.

Figure 31.5 Cabin

We dove on the Cabin Wreck and found something awesome! It was a cannon. We then built a fiberglass box then transported it to Amelia Island Florida. (With permission from the Florida Bureau of Archaeological Research of course!).

The cannon was iron and would need to go through the process of electrolysis to clean it. A wrecker was used to transport it on site to the museum. The following photographs are the author getting encrustation off the cannon.

Figure 32   Taking the encrustation off

Figure 33   Treasure Cannon

A decision was to be made not to put cannon through electrolysis as the water would be cloudy. We filled the fiberglass tank with water and put a circulation pump the to keep the water clear. That worked amazingly well!

❧ CHAPTER FIVE ❧

Two Islands

THERE ARE TWO ISLANDS IN Jacksonville Florida called Big Talbot and Little Talbot. On Big Talbot you are not allowed to metal detect, on Little Talbot Island you can. What's up? Humm, I think the Florida State Park is there to protect something on Big Talbot. It not the environment, people hike Big Talbot by the thousands!

Our team metal detected Little Talbot Island and found around 600 coins some new, some old, and some where really old! Lots of trash, beer cans and anything you can imagine!

In the following the reader will see some of the treasure author found on the island!

Figure 34   New Coins found on Little Talbot Island

Figure 35   Old Coins of Little Talbot Island

Figure 36   Finding Gold

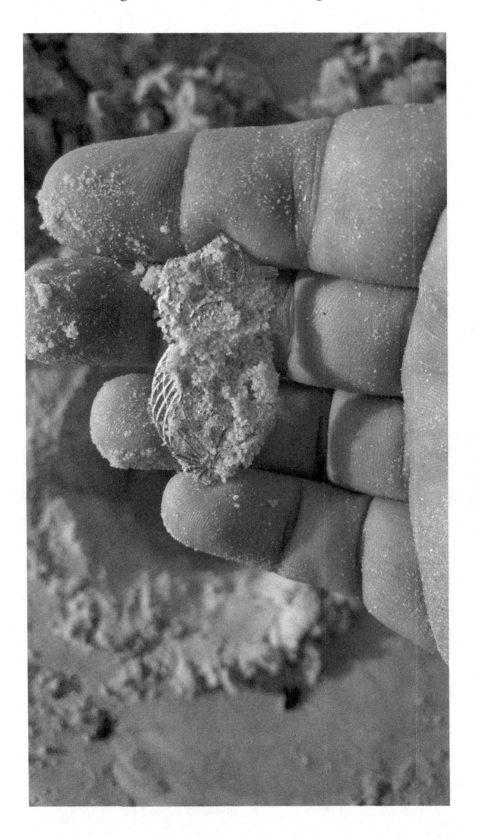

Figure 37   Gold Emblem

Figure 37.1   Section of 1800 Vessel

⚜ CHAPTER SIX ⚜

Treasure on Amelia Island

AMELIA ISLAND IS RICH IN archeological sites, to date there are over 65 on record. Most archaeological sites do not translate into treasure. However, that being said, I will concentrate on some of the treasures sites on Amelia Island located in Nassau County Florida. You cannot talk about Amelia Island without the towns called Old Fernandina / New Fernandina.

The public assumes no treasure has been found on Amelia Island. Some believe there was never any treasure on the island; believe the author, they are **wrong.**

"Is there treasure on Amelia Island?" Yes, there

is. How much is yet to be determined!

Figure 38 Amelia Island

<u>Old Fernandina / New Fernandina</u>

This was taken from the original *Amelia Island Book of Secrets* that I wrote after 25 years of exploration, and talking to people, but never published. Notice on the map above, New Fernandina is located in the confines of the area south of Old Fernandina. On the map provided by *The Maritime Museum of Amelia Island Archives* Figure 38, there were very few roads on the island. Today, there are nearly 2000 roads on Amelia Island. I will start with the original of town Fernandina.

A massive boardwalk through the marshlands connected Old Fernandina and New Fernandina. There was no road access going to Old Fernandina. According to *Yesterday Reflections* the map in Old Fernandina and New Fernandina was connected through the marshlands by a boardwalk.

Figure 39   Boardwalk

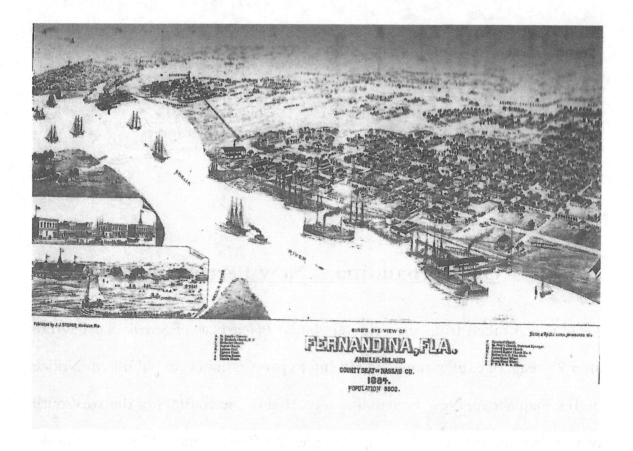

This area is now called Old Town; at one time it was called Old Fernandina. (the original Fernanda). Figure 40 is a map drawn in the original *Book of Secrets*; the map was from 1821 with updates from other maps circa 1784.

I personally visited with several residents from Old Town. Many of the residents had dug up coquina steps underground, seeming to go nowhere. Supposedly the steps led to a tunnel with the purpose of residents escaping to Fort San Carlos. Many people believe the tunnel is under Egan's Creek, as an archaeologist, I can assure you that is not possible.

Figure 41 shows a cross on the ground near the main gate, it will explain why and how it was constructed. Even though the cross does not exist today, construction workers found it in early 1800's.

The workers were building what is now known as N 14th Street. That gave the first road access to Old Town (Old Fernandina).

Figure 40   A map of Old Town

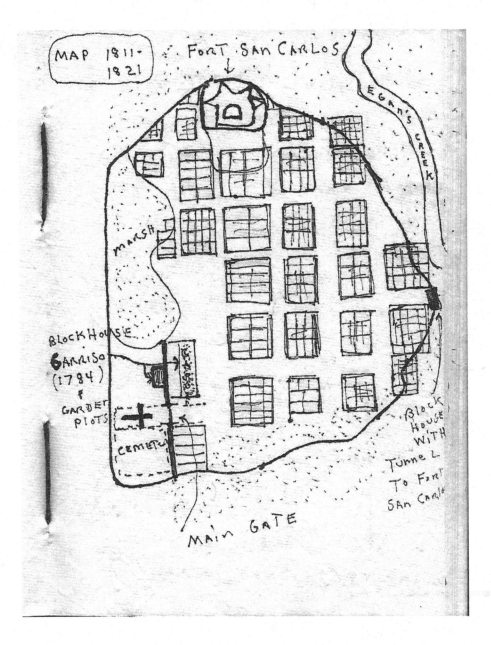

Figure 41 Fragments of the City Gates

* CITY GATES.: FRAGMENTS OF
FOUNDATION ARE VISABLE.
DURNING the BUILDING OF
14TH STREET WORKMEN UN EARTHED
A TRENCH in the FORM OF
A CROSS, 18 FEET Long, 3 FEET
WIDE, AND 2 FEET DEEP.
FILLED WITH OYSTER SHELL

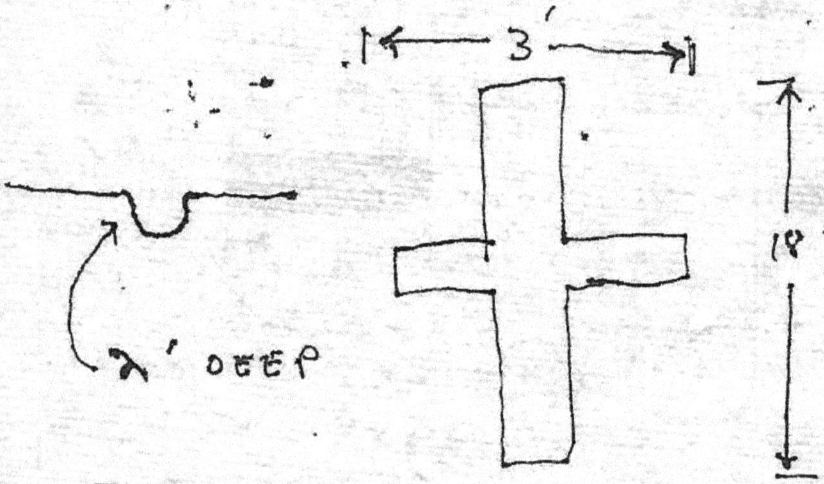

2' DEEP

3'

18'

IT MARKS CONSECRATED GROUND

These series of photos are from a coin that was found in Old Fernandina (Old Town). The coin depicts King Ferdinand VII who died in 1833. Old Fernandina was named after the King. Look closely at the pictures of the coin as the date is 1833.

Figure 42   Coin

Figure 43　　　　　Coin 2

Figure 44   Coin 3

Figure 44.5   Egan's Creek & surrounding areas

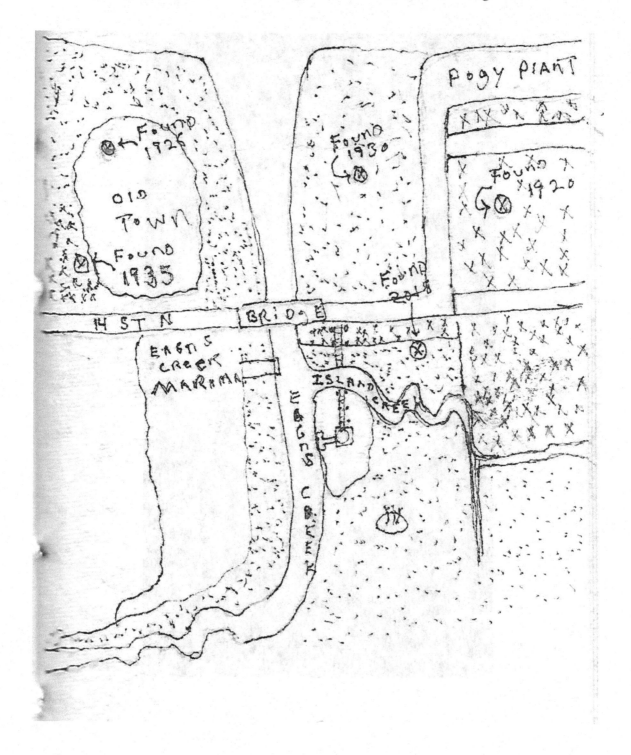

Figure 44.7   The Florida Times–Union on Monday, November 25, 1935.

The Florida Times-Union

JACKSONVILLE, FLORIDA, MONDAY, NOVEMBER 25, 1935.

Pirate Gold Believed to Be Buried on Amelia Island Is Lure for Treasure Hunters

T. Howard Kelly, Writer, Is Organizer of Group That Will Make Search.

Pirate gold will lure a group of "gentlemen adventurers" to Amelia Island, where shortly after the first of the year they will begin their quest for the doubloons of buccaneers, who tradition says, found the Barrier Islands off the Northeast Florida coast an excellent hiding place for their loot as early as the latter part of the Seventeenth century.

T. Howard Kelly, noted writer, who calls Fernandina his home, is the organizer of what he calls the Amelia Island Pirate Treasure Expedition, and announced the purpose of the explorations while a visitor here Saturday.

Mr. Kelly said the following prominent persons are interested in the expedition.

Bradshaw Crandell, Cosmopolitan Magazine cover artist; John Charles Thomas, famous baritone; George Angue Dobyns, retired capitalist of Easton, Md., and Palm Beach; Jay Hyde Barnum, noted illustrator for Colliers, American Magazine, Pictorial Review and Cosmopolitan; Kimbark Howell, New London and Palm Beach yachtsman; Robert Ferguson and Carter Carnegie of Cumberland Island, Ga.; George Fenton, Buffalo and Palm Beach sportsman; Bill Berri, New York City and Miami yachtsman; Dan Kelly Jr., legislator and attorney of Fernandina, and others.

Mr. Kelly who divides his time between Florida and the East, has been spending November in the State perfecting plans for the treasure expedition and attending to other business. Most of those interested in the explorations for the treasure became attracted to the venture while visiting Mr. Kelly at his beach house on Amelia Island last Spring, he said.

"From 1683 to 1685, a pirate named Agramont, who became notorious as 'Abraham', plundered, burned and scourged what is now St. Catherine's Island above Sapelo Island, and continued his depredations down to Amelia Island.

Used By Blackbeard.

"Later, in 1715, Thomas Leache, famous as Blackbeard, used the island, now known on the United States maps as Blackbeard Island, for a base. He even extended his operations as far down as Little Talbot Island, using the harbor of Fernandina.

"Luis Aury, another buccaneer, took Amelia Island in 1817, and there tried to establish a republic, after erecting the flag of Mexico.

"Gradually, the section, on account of being close to deep water, became a popular rendezvous for pirates."

The most direct information concerning pirate treasure is connected with the story of Captain Kidd, according to Mr. Kelly. There are residents on Amelia Island today, he related, whose fathers and grandfathers have told them a story of the four expeditions made by the famous buccaneer and his terrorizing marauders, sailing in and out of the harbor at what is now Fernandina.

So the story goes, when Captain Kidd visited Amelia Island on his last trip, he anchored off shore, and sent every member of his crew into the jungle thickets with treasure, which, it is said, they buried in a designated spot.

The narrators of this quaint and exciting lore say that after he had caused the doubloons to be cached, he ordered the majority of his crew killed on the spot, or had them cast overboard at sea. This left only him and his chosen few conspirators with a knowledge of the coveted fortune in pirate gold.

Since that time, 20 expeditions are reported to have made hunts for the treasure of Blackbeard and Amelia Islands.

Figure 44.9   Pirate Gold by T. Howard Kelly (Courtesy of the Cloyd Family)

Vho Think—SUNDAY, DECEMBER 22, 1935   E—3

Buried Pirate Gold Lures Expedition To Amelia Island Jungles Off Florida

Expedition to Hunt Treasure Cached by Capt. Kidd and 17th Century Buccaneers

By T. HOWARD KELLY,

Author of "What Outfit Buddy!" "The Unknown Soldier"— "Lovers' Island"—"Enchanted Dusk," and Other Books and Stories.

SOMETIME within the next few weeks, John Charles Thomas, acting as Commodore of our Amelia Island Pirate Treasure Expedition's yacht fleet, will break out a black and white pirate flag from the signal mast of his flagship Masquerader in the picturesque harbor of Fernandina, Florida.

Thereupon some 20 members of our company of gentlemen adventurers will assemble on the Masquerader's quarterdeck to receive final orders concerning our forthcoming plunge into the almost impenetrable jungles of historic, palm-fringed Amelia Island, which lies just off the northeastern mainland of Florida.

In its tangled thickets of pines, Spanish bayonets, oaks, palmettoes and cabbage palms we will conduct an intensive and systematic search for chests of buccaneer gold and gems which history, tradition and legend maintain were secretly cached there by Agramont, Captain Kidd, Blackbeard, Luis Aury and other cutthroat sea bandits.

victed, and hanged as history relates.

Ever so often the discovery of an anchor chain fastened to an Amelia Island jungle oak is reported. But I am convinced that Kidd did not leave such an obvious marker for his buried treasure. If I am not badly mistaken, Kidd's cache is in the area we intend searching.

About 35 years ago, two Negroes named Goss and Pinkney stumbled across a partly buried iron chest in Amelia's southeastern jungle. It contained approximately $20,000 in 17th and 18th century coins. Pinkney was subsequently reported on the mainland. But Goss dropped out of sight and mysterious stories of tragedy

Treasure has always been in Old Town and the surrounding areas; on numerous occasions coins have been unearthed. According to an *Unknown Text* (partial text) surmised to be from the early 1950's, in 1920 a black man named Tray found a pot of silver coins near Fort Clinch.

In 1926, a man found an old can of silver coins at Fort San Carlos. He then took the proceeds and purchased a house on the West Coast of Florida.

In the early thirties (1930's), two black men found a cache of gold coins between Old Town and Fort Clinch. They were 400 coins in all, dating back as far as the 1500's. They were of Spanish, French and English coinage.

An inventory of all the coins they found is listed on the following page. This find is impressive.....................

- Spanish Double Excellentes (1500's)

- French (1600)

- Spanish Double Ducats (1560's)

- French Double Louis (1644)

- English (1640's) 400 coins is a very impressive find from the 1500's to mid-1600's.

In another occurrence approximately twenty years later, a child was making mud pies near Bosque Bellow (translated in Spanish is Beautiful Woods) Cemetery and discovered coins.

Her father came out of the house and helped the child dig the hole. The youngster had uncovered a Spanish pot with $18,000.00 of silver coins in it. This was in the 1935 in Old Fernandina.

In 2018, a cache of treasure coins was found in a chest in the Old Town area. I sought out the person who found the cache and located the successful treasure hunter. He took me to a vault location that I will keep secret. I physically touched the case, its contents; I was amazed at what I was looking at. I was looking into the face of history.

He said when the chest was pulled out of the ground it crumbled. All was not lost; he glued the chest together as best as he could. There was no hardware on the chest; no hinges, no skeleton key hardware and no pins to hold it together.

This treasure hunter would not allow me to photograph the chest and as a successful archeologist myself I do not blame him. This treasure finder was smart. It would bring undo attention to his amazing find, and people would try to claim it.

He allowed me to conduct a quick inventory of the chest and it contained beautiful pieces. It contained gold coins, silver coins, rings, emeralds and gold nuggets. It contained a bronze crucifix, which I found interesting, it contained the head of a Mayan / Aztec / Incan. All the coins were from the 1500's to the 1700's. This is what I saw……………..

- 2 Silver Rings
- 2 Gold Doubloons

- 23 Gold Nuggets

- 2 Emeralds

- 119 Silvers Coins

- 1 Crucifix

- 2 Containers

- 1 Chest Wood with skeleton key hole. Disintegrated upon pulling it out of the ground.

Assume the chest is 1700's?

I was very appreciative of the gentleman for allowing

me to physically examine his treasure!

Included in this section of **Treasure of Amelia Island** are newspaper articles of more treasures found on the island. According to *The New York Times* published May 28 1897, a black man found treasure on Amelia Island. In fact, different groups had discovered $45,000.00 in two finds of Spanish gold.

Several people were in a group looking for the treasure. The black man followed them to their treasure cache and took their map and charts. Supposedly they could not find the site again and vacated the island.

The black man took the maps and charts and found what he was looking for. He found the treasure containing over $39,000.00 in Spanish gold. The newspaper reported amateur treasurers' hunters that coins had dug been up four acres at or around the base of trees!

Can you imagine finding a cache of $39,000.00 in 1897? Amelia Island had many plantations on it. The 1897 salary was based on a farmer's salary. The average monthly income was $19.00. According to *Measuring Worth*, the treasure would be worth well over a $1,000, 000.00 in today's value!

Figure 45   Article from the New York Times published 1897

BURIED GOLD IN FLORIDA

Alleged Recovery of $45,000 in Old Spanish Doubloons on Amelia Island, Near Fernandina.

FERNANDINA, Fla., May 27.—Within the past few months $45,000 have been unearthed on Amelia Island, near this city, consisting of two finds of gold doubloons of the Spanish Government. They have created a sensation. In both instances the searches were conducted very secretly and the money was taken away before the truth was made known.

The first find was $6,000, and was made some months ago by a party of strangers posing as scientists. They were here over a month, and left suddenly after some charts they had were stolen by a negro, they claimed. This person, Chris Pinckney, a keen, sharp-witted darky, overheard them talking of their plans, and one night he followed them, and saw them dig up a box. When they opened it he saw the gleam of gold coins, and heard them say that there was over $6,000 in it. The next day he took French leave, and with him disappeared their charts.

Some weeks after they were gone Pinckney reappeared. He went to work for George Gause, a lumberman. Gause was kind to him in some sickness, and to him the negro showed the papers. Gause was incredulous at first, but finally took hold of the matter with Pinckney, with the result, as now ascertained, that they found a box containing a large amount of old Spanish doubloons, variously estimated at from $32,000 to $39,000. This was in April.

They would not dispose of the money here for fear that some one might claim it. Pinckney finally said he would go to Savannah and Brunswick, Ga., and change it into bills. Gause acceded, and he sold out his plant here, as he intended going West with his share. But Pinckney disappeared, and finally Gause came to the conclusion that his partner had gone with the money. He went to Lawyer W. A. Hall and stated the case.

On a promise of one-quarter of the amount recovered, Hall took the case. On May 3 he went to Tallahassee and secured a commission from Gov. Bloxham empowering him to hunt for buried treasure at a percentage of one-half. Search was then made for Pinckney. He was located in New York City, but the police, though wired to, could not find him. After waiting for some time, Gause stated that he would go after him, as he felt confident of finding him.

Gause left here May 14, but up to date has not been heard from, and consequently Lawyer Hall is rather "hot under the collar." He thinks now that Gause has used him as a "stool-pigeon." His opinion is that Gause found Pinckney in New York and that the men divided the treasure there. Rather than come back and divide with Hall, Gause, according to Hall's idea, left for the West or for Central America. Anyway, Hall is after him, and has wired the police in several cities to look out for him.

The find is no myth, as Hall saw some of the money and was shown the hole where it was found, under a big oak tree on Amelia Island, the bottom of the excavation showing the form of the box taken out. Then, too, Gause paid out several hundred dollars here before going, in doubloons, and many merchants have these old coins.

The town is greatly excited over the matter, and amateur treasure seekers are at work daily digging around old trees on the island. Over four acres in one place have been dug over in this way.

The main facts came to light only yesterday, and then by accident, as Hall has been keeping quiet, hoping to get some news from Gause. The truth of the story is so well established here that it has carried the place by storm.

The New York Times
Published: May 28, 1897

This article was taken from the *News-Leader*, this paper was first published in 1854. It is recognized as the oldest weekly newspaper in Florida. This article was published in October 31,1924.

In the following article, it describes a gentleman who found coins on Amelia Island. This started a gold rush on the island with people digging on the island with picks and shovels. Like others before him, he found them in Old Town.

Figure 46   Discovery of Gold

DISCOVERY OF GOLD NEAR FERNANDINA SETS FOLKS TO WORK WITH SHOVELS AND PICKS

NEGRO FISHERMAN UNEARTHS QUANTITY OF SPANISH DOUBLOONS MINTED MORE THAN 100 YEARS AGO.

The following from the Nassau County Leader tells an interesting story, linking Florida with the early doings of the Spanish buccaneers. It reads:

That fishermen at times have luck ashore, as well as at sea, is proved by the fact that Robt. Cribb, colored, of the shrimp boat "Republic," owned by Frank Graham, of Fernandina, has recently been exhibiting ancient Spanish silver coins which he found on this island last week.

Fisherman Cribb, who lives at Old Town, brought some coins to Mr. Graham last Saturday and asked as to their identity and probable value, stating that the recent heavy rains have washed down a bank near Old Town and that he dug the coins out at the edge of the cavern.

Those he exhibited to Mr. Graham were of silver and a trifle larger than our U. S. silver dollar but not quite as thick, and they probably contain about the same amount of silver as the U. S. dollar.

One of the coins is dated 1796 and has on its face a likeness of Carolus Fourth, King of Spain. Others bear the likeness of Ferdinand Seventh, king of Spain. All the coins are over a hundred years old and still they show no signs of hard usage. All the letters of the inscriptions on both the obverse and reverse sides of the money are

as plain and easily read as when they were minted. Also they are almost as bright and untarnished as when new.

The fisherman who found them is not communicative as to how many he secured, nor will he state definitely where the caved bank is located, except to say that it is near Old Town, and not far from Fort Clinch. No one blames him for his reticence. The find is his find.

Members of old-time families now resident at Old Town tell tales handed down to them from their great-grandparents, of how Amelia Island was, a hundred years ago, a famous rendezvous for the pirates of the Spanish Main, and they will to this day show visitors the rotted timbers of an ancient dock at Old Town where they say their ancestors claimed the pirates made their landings. Has Fisherman Cribb found buried pirate treasure or is the money a relic of the Spanish occupation of this island?

The coins are too bright and too nearly "mint proof" to have been carelessly lost by some one. Their fine condition leads to the inference that they had been carefully packed away.

Cribb gave one of the older coins to his employer, Mr. Frank Graham, who brought it to the Leader office for exhibition to any one interested.

The news of this find has aroused once more the ambition of the many Ferdinand treasure hunters who are wise to the fact that one fortune in gold doubloons

Talking to the old-timers they told the author about another treasure from the late 1800's. It was a story where three men were on the hunt with a map. According to the old-timers one man died and the other two men continued on.

The group told me that the two men found a hole in the in the back of the creek (Egan's Creek?) and more is still there. The story goes that the two remaining men found $170,000.00 in gold and jewels. The Port of Call for the vessel that transported the treasure was New York.

$170,000.00 in gold and silver the treasure would be worth roughly $4,000,000.00 dollars today. The author cannot confirm this but Amelia Island has many stories!

Figures 47 and 48 are a letter sent to the *Fernandina Chamber of Commerce* describing a gentleman's search for treasure on Amelia Island in 1934.

Figure 47   Letter

February 3, 1934.

Dear Madam:

   Your letter of January 29th addressed to the Postmaster of Fernandina, Florida, has been referred to us for reply.

   During the period from 1680 to 1763 Cumberland Sound and Amelia River was a harbor of rendezvous for slave traders and pirates. In 1763 the peninsular of Florida was ceded, by Spain, to England and under English rule this lawless element did not find favorable operating conditions, hence they abandoned the use of the harbor. In 1784 the peninsular was ceded back to Spain and from then on until 1817 was again a favorite harbor for free booters. During these two periods it has been assumed that treasure was buried by pirates on the Island. We do not know of any actual instance of treasure having been found except that in 1928 or 1929 a small quantity of ancient coins were turned up during excavation.

   In the neighborhood of the beach is a long narrow stretch of hammock land and on this tract an old negro lived for many years, named Uncle Jimmie Drummond. He was called a Seminole Indian but long time residents here say he was a full blooded negro. He was, however, a very unique character. He habitually kept a pen of rattle snakes and had a reputation among the colored people here of being able to conjure. The legend is that somewhere on the tract of land on which he lived there was buried treasure and that near that treasure was an oak tree with an old iron chain hanging in the tree and grown into it. The legend further states that on dark nights the chain will be rattled by spirit hands and no one had the courage to excavate for this treasure for fear of death at the hands of these guardian spirits. Uncle Jimmie died last year.

Figure 48   Letter 2

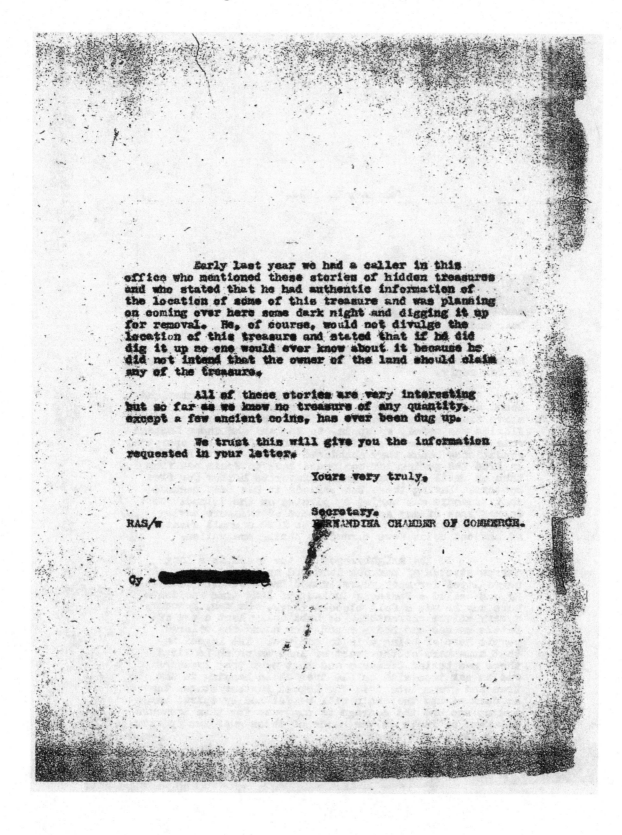

Early last year we had a caller in this office who mentioned these stories of hidden treasures and who stated that he had authentic information of the location of some of this treasure and was planning on coming over here some dark night and digging it up for removal. He, of course, would not divulge the location of this treasure and stated that if he did dig it up no one would ever know about it because he did not intend that the owner of the land should claim any of the treasure.

All of these stories are very interesting but so far as we know no treasure of any quantity, except a few ancient coins, has ever been dug up.

We trust this will give you the information requested in your letter.

Yours very truly,

Secretary.
FERNANDINA CHAMBER OF COMMERCE.

RAS/w

Cy -

Gold Rush in New Fernandina

A cache of gold bars was found at a site in New Fernandina in 1976. According to the Fernandina Beach Court House (which displays one of the bars) it caused so much commotion in the city that they dispatched the police to guard the find.

People were raiding the site as the word of the find spread around the town. They were coming into the city with shovels, pick axes and whatever tools they could get at the treasure with. Little did they know Deputies were guarding the cache of gold bars.

After the excitement had subsided (Deputies still on guard), one gold bar was sent to the University of Florida. Ouch! The bars were not gold at all. The university determined it was not gold, but a bar with alloys in it.

The site was found when bulldozers where cleaning out land for a new Department of Health. Low and behold the previous land had a metal producing building on it. The building was long gone and so are the gold bars. I can only find ¾ of a bar displayed at the courthouse at Fernandina Beach on Center Street.

Figure 49   Gold Bars found in New Fernandina

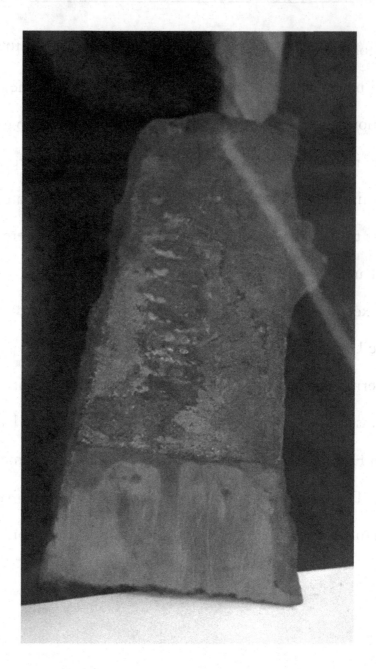

Figure 50   Gold Bars found on New Fernandina 2

Artifacts & Ocean

By land or sea there **is** treasure on Amelia Island Florida, you just have to look for it! I will show you in this section the Atlantic Ocean and all its glory. The ocean can be angry with waves taller than houses or it can be flat like a sheet of ice.

As an archeologist I will explain to you how a Spanish Galleon becomes a shipwreck. A Spanish Galleon can survive a hurricane if they are in deep water (not always but the majority of the time). When the ships skirted the coast and a hurricane or a northeaster hits (remember they did not have weather forecasting at the time) that was when the trouble started.

A fully loaded 1715 Galleon had approximately an 18-foot draft (the draft is the water line of the ship to the bottom of the Galleon) if you have a 35-foot crest (crest is the highest part of the wave) with a trough (trough is the lowest part of the wave) of 19 feet, the ship will hit the bottom and crack like an egg.

The deck would shear off and surf to the shore like a surf board. The bottom would fall where it hit and all was lost. Contained in the ship were ballast stones, silver bars and boxes of silver coins, gold coins and jewelry.

The authors group had the chance to go on private property near the Atlantic Ocean and search. Our group found 210 pins, spikes, tacks and miscellaneous items. These items were made of iron and bronze and would be used to hold the ship together. Also discovered were Spanish coins and a French ring made of silver.

Looking at Figure 51 our group excavated these pins, spikes and tacks. This was about 50% of the artifacts we discovered.

Figure 51 Spikes & Pins

Four Spikes, notice the U.S. quarter to put the size in perspective.

Notice how they are bent by the massive power of the Atlantic Ocean

Figure 52

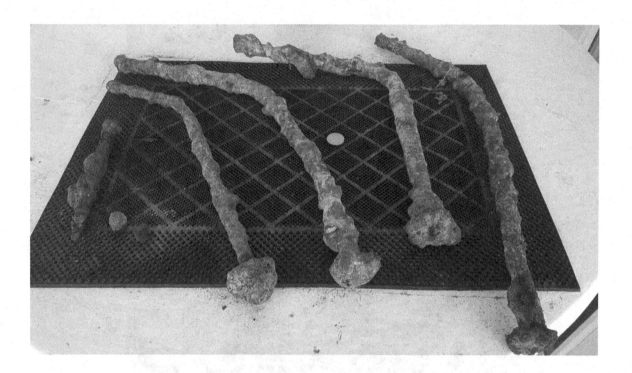

Figure 53   Spikes and pins out of the 210 our group found

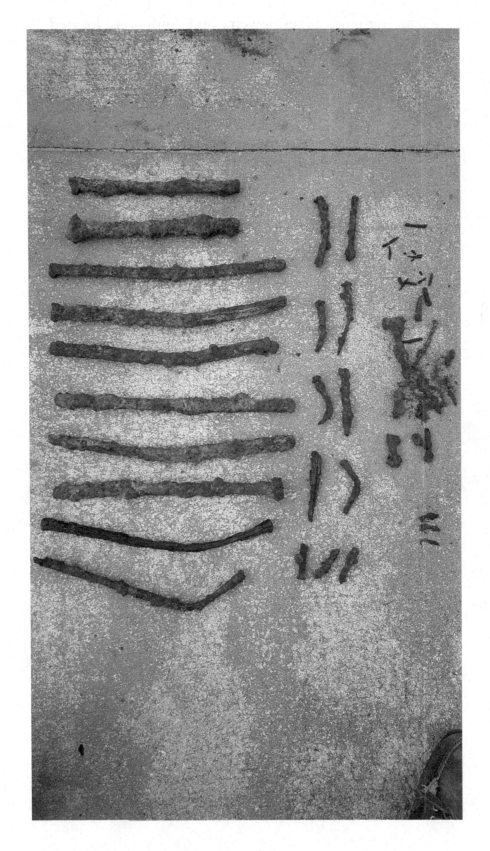

These are the log sheets that the author created to determine

where the pins, spikes, jewelry and coins were located

Figure 54

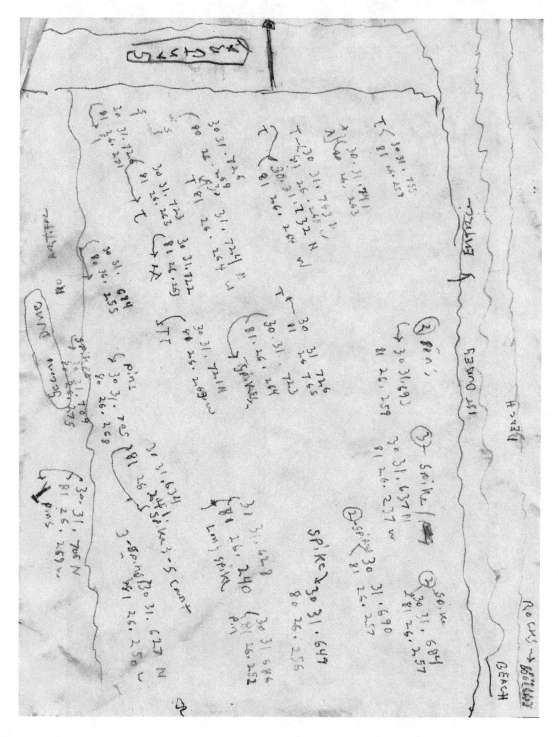

The second log sheet from the South End of Amelia Island

Figure 55

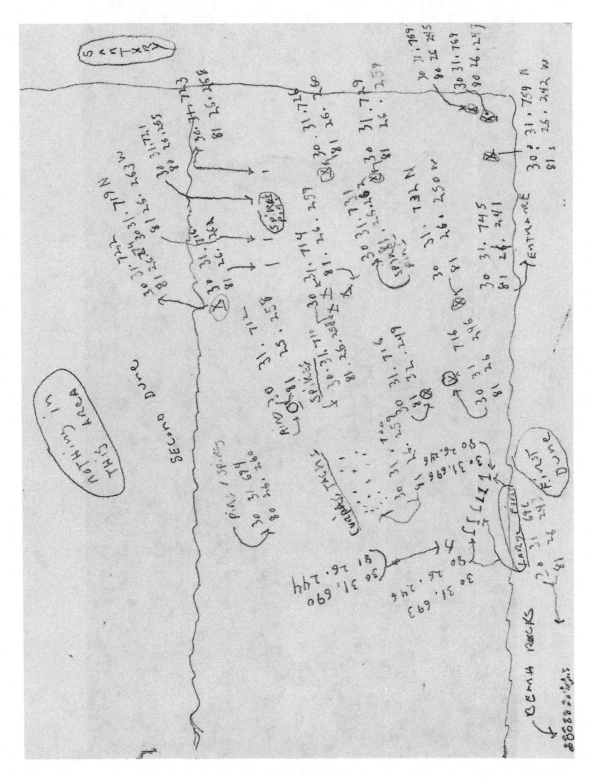

Figure 56   Spanish Coins found on Amelia Island

This is a small piece of wood with spikes in it, located in

the same area as the coins, spikes, pins and jewelry

Figure 57

Figure 58   A French Ring discovered by the author

Figure 59   The author holds up a coin he excavated

Figure 60　　　　　Two Spanish coins found by a member of our team

Figure 61   The author holding a coin

The author took this picture in 1978. A massive keel and rib that washed in

from the beach. The keel runs along the bottom in the center of the ship

Figure 62

Eugene Lyon Ph.D. was a Historian and was the foremost expert of Spanish history in the world. He lived in St Augustine Florida and headed the Department of History at Flagler Collage. Lyons went to the Archives in Seville Spain and found many shipwrecks on the East Coast.

On April 28th 2018 he gave me permission to include some of his documents in *Amelia Island Book of Secrets*. He died shortly thereafter. These are two of his documents.

Figure 63   Lyon Papers

EUGENE LYON. Ph.D.

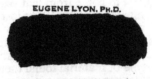

April 13, 1994

Please find attached:

1. A report on the two vessels from the 1715 <u>Tierra Firme</u> fleet which were evidently never salvaged, and which may in fact be the source of the coins you have found in your work area.

2. Also sent along is a summary of Florida documents which relate to the 1715 business, one of which describes the trip "north" at some date prior to November, 1715, when one of the Florida Treasury officials, Francisco Menéndez Marquéz, made the voyage to check out the matter. I also examined the Florida accounts (Archives of the Indies[hereinafter AGI] <u>Contaduría</u> 952), but found no entry for the trip.

3. Along with these I send a copy of a document from AGI <u>Consulados</u>, which describes the shipwrecks and the personnel losses on each vessel. I translated the general part and those which refer to the two ships <u>San Miguel</u> and <u>Ciervo.</u>

Since the accounts gave no further clue or evidence, I think the best immediate follow-up for me is to trace the Virginia Governor's story, which implies information arriving in Willamsburg about the north Florida shipwrecks.

This is an exciting business, which may yield some good results. Please advise when and how I can help. With best personal wishes, I am

Yours sincerely,

Eugene Lyon

Figure 64   Lyon Papers 2

Report on 1715 Shipwrecks north of St. Augustine

Generally, the locations of the 1715 losses are pretty well known, with some notable exceptions. Unfortunately, no definitive identification has been made on any of the known shipwrecks, but some of the sites are tentatively identified. The early survivors stated that they knew where all the ships had wrecked except for four; the Concepción, the San Miguel, the French prize and the Grifon. This is so stated by the chief pilot of Ubilla's fleet, Captain Nicolás de Ynda, in a letter dated from Havana on 16 August 1715 and found in AGI Santo Domingo 419. As we know, Grifon escaped to return safely to France. Up to the date of that report, the survivors always had said the ships were ten leagues (almost 35 n.m. apart, @ 3.44 n.m. to a league), lying from 27 d. 15' to 27 d 50'. After that point, they said the wrecks were 15 or 16 leagues apart. You can only add those extra leagues to the north, for the southernmost of the wrecks was clearly Miguel de Lima's urca, the Santísima Trinidad. This designation of Lima's ship as the southernmost site never changed during the years of Spanish salvage up to 1719, when effective work on the sites ceased.

On the north end of the known wrecks immediately after the hurricane ceased, the New Spain Almiranta was located at 27 d 50', almost precisely the location of the Cabin Wreck. That shipwreck has yielded the type of coins (Mexico mint)and the kind of personal and religious jewelry and artifacts one might expect to come from that vessel. Moreover, it is quite logical that the other New Spain capital ship, the Capitana, was lost ca. two leagues to the south. This corresponds with the "Corrigan's" site. In fact, the testimony of one Pedro de la Vega makes it certain that the Almiranta of Ubilla's fleet and its camp were located north of that of his Capitana, for as the English raiders came down upon the latter camp, Spaniards fled southward along the beach. Again, the type of material found there, with a New Spain provenience, would correspond with a large, passenger-carrying capital vessel from Vera Cruz. It is evident, moreover, that the salvage camp of the patache of New Spain was located some distance to the southward of the two New Spain capital ships, since one observer, Pedro de la Vega, required the time from 7 p.m. to 3 a.m. to arrive at the patache camp(Testimony of Pedgo de la Vega, AGI Escribanía de Cámara 55-C, fol. 111vto.), which in turn was located some two leagues to the north of the southernmost of the New Spain shipwreck sites, that of the ship of Miguel de Lima.Lima himself says that his ship was "the first, which is towards the upper Keys (from the rest)" (AGI Santo Domingo 419).

This leaves the Concepción, a few survivors of which came ashore on raft somewhere north of the Sebastian inlet, and the San Miguel and the Ciervo. It is easy to confuse the two ships which bore the name of San Miguel. It is evident that the lost one was the larger vessel, which had sailed all the way from Spain with Echevers, and its data follows:

San Miguel

A frigate, Vizcayan built. 180 3/4 tons; 22 cannons, 18 4-pounders and 4 two-pounders. Her beam was 22.5', her keel length 72', and her overall length was 83'.. Master is Joesph Coyto de Melo; he was among the sixty two persons drowned as the ship was lost with all hands. Also included in the lost personnel were Don Domingo and Don Tomás Moynos, citizens of Cádiz, Don Joseph Tamorlan, Guardian Jacome de Noblería, Pilot Alonso de Silvestre and Quartermaster Domingo de Yguzquiza. 22 sailors, 24 grommets and four pages were lost. Not to be confused with another San Miguel, a sloop prize captured by Echeverz in the Caribbean and likely disposed of in Havana. The larger San Miguel may be the vessel reported lost north of St. Augustine. She carried tobacco from Havana and was a "registry" vessel, evidently from Cádiz; that is, it had special permission for lading by merchants from that city.

Page 1

100

Remember when the author told you that the deck shears off and surfs to the shore? That is exactly what this ship has done. What is age of this ship? It could be 1600s to the 1800s, however, with that being said, the Spanish coins and jewelry found on the site tend to suggest it is a Spanish ship in origin.

Spikes, pins, coins and jewelry can only mean one thing, a shipwreck. I surmise that these could the shipwrecks of the *San Miguel* or the *Ciervo*. These ships sank in the 1715 Plate Fleet. (Plate means **treasure**).

So, what does this all mean? It is my perception there is a least one (or more) Colonial Period (1607 to 1776) shipwreck's in the Nassau Sound or International waters. The evidence supports the theory that shipwrecks are in this area.

This map was drawn by Lou Ullian of the *Real Eight Company* in the 1960's and 1970's from memory. Graciously, I have permission to use this map by Helen Ullian and Rex Stocker, the surviving members of the company.

The *Real Eight Company* was the first company to find and salvage Spanish shipwrecks on the coast of Florida. Eventually they came to Amelia Island. On Amelia Island, they found many gold and silver coins. On Talbot Island there were more coins. Here is Lou Ullian's Map of Amelia and Talbot Island...

Figure 65   Map

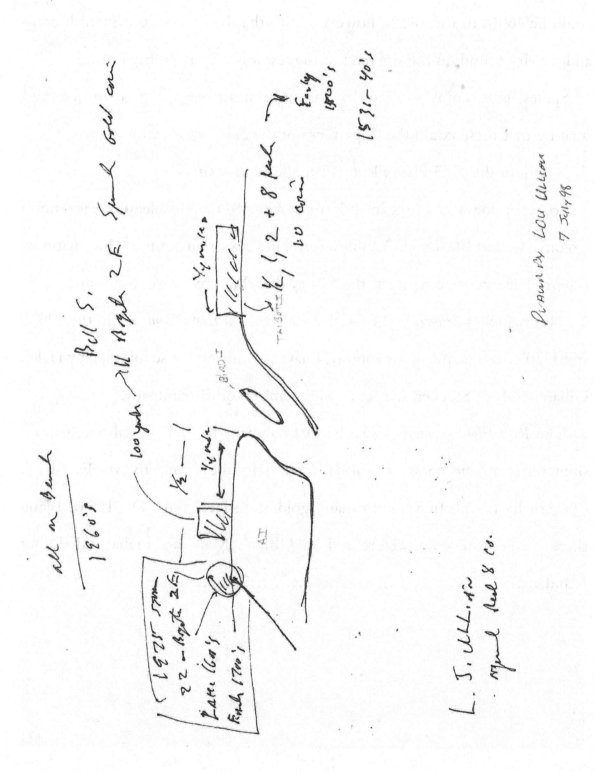

Lou Ullian's handwritten map shows where the *Real Eight Company* found treasure on the beach and in the Atlantic Ocean.

<u>Amelia Island Florida in 1960's</u>.

11 Bogotá 2 Escudos Spanish (gold) Coins

<u>Talbot Island Florida</u>

10 Spanish Reales (silver) Coins

Early 1500's

1531–1540's

<u>Amelia Island in 1975</u>

22 Bogota 2 Escudos Spanish (gold) Coins

Early 1600's

Early 1700's

The author coming out of the Atlantic Ocean with

dive gear one mile off of Amelia Island

Figure 66

Figure 67   Colonial Period coin found by the author

❧ CHAPTER SEVEN ❧

The Amelia Island Lighthouse

ACROSS FROM AMELIA ISLAND THERE is an island called Cumberland, the thing that separates the two islands is an inlet. This is an island were horses that run free, the Carnegies had a mansion that burned down, John F Kennedy Jr was married in a little Chapel. The island has a small piece of privately owned land containing a Bed & Breakfast inn.

This Lighthouse was built on Cumberland Island in Georgia in 1820. A problem began, the Lighthouse began sinking. Some people think they did not survey it correctly, others think it was sinking, still others think the channel was shifting.

Whatever the true story, it was sinking and it was not visible to the maritime ships to guide them to the inlet. (St Mary's River). It took an "Act of Congress" to get the funding to move it.

Cumberland Island was known to have shipwrecks and treasures of all types. When they moved the lighthouse, there was said to be treasure found nearby. These stories were passed down for generations of families. What do you think?

In the last twenty years two shipwreck (I surmise that it the same shipwreck) were discovered during a storm and recently a garment chest washed up on the beaches of Cumberland. A shipwreck (supposedly) is located on Pelican Shoal (Pelican Shoal is of a patch of water near Cumberland) that is said to be one of the oldest in in the New World!

There is a nuclear Naval Base in Georgia and the submarines go thru the inlet. If you stay to long in a fishing boat you will be surrounded by Navy vessels with personnel standing on the deck with M-16's. Their mission is not to protect Pelican Shoal, but to protect the submarines.

Figure 68   Submarine going toward through the Inlet

In 1838 the lighthouse was disassembled block by block and moved to

Amelia Island. The lighthouse was reassembled on Egan Creek in 1839! (New Fernandina).

Figure 69   Reassembled Lighthouse on Amelia Island

Figure 70 The lighthouse today is on a bluff standing on 60 feet above the water

The lighthouse is 67 feet tall and the location protects it from hurricanes, northeastern winds and storms. When the lighthouse was moved from Cumberland Island to Amelia Island it was built with a light keeper's house. Sadly, this house no longer exists.

As for the treasure, I found modern coins and a one-dollar American bill! After thousands of dives, walk abouts to find artifacts, I have resigned myself to walked the Amelia Island beaches!

Figure 71   Close up of the Lighthouse

⚜ CHAPTER EIGHT ⚜

Enjoyment!

Figure 72   The author standing in front a replica Spanish Galleon

I WAS AT A FRIEND'S HOUSE in my truck, and my girlfriend came over and left a note under my windshield wiper blades. The note simply said that "You live day by day; I can't do that and you will never change".

Thinking about it now, she was right. She wanted children, most people live vicariously thru their children eyes, I couldn't do that. I wanted to experience my life. I love the water, the sand and everything that goes with it; after 4 college degrees, I became a Maritime Archaeologist. In my short life I hope she is happy, because I am!

MY EYES HAVE SEEN WONDERFUL THINGS!

REFERENCES CITED

Buried Pirate Gold Lures Expedition to Amelia Island Jungles Off Florida New York American, Sunday, December 22, 1935

Buried Gold in Florida, The New York Times May 28, 1897.

Cabin. The Martine Museum of Amelia Island Archives, Fernandina Beach, Florida. 1960.

Fernandina Chamber of Commerce
Unpublished Letter February 3, 1934

Discovery of Gold Near Fernandina, News-Leader October 31, 1928.

Lyons, Eugene, Personal Communication.

Johannes, Jan. Yesterday's Reflections, (Preface) Lexington Ventures Inc. Fernandina Beach, Florida. 2000.

Map. The Maritime Museum of Amelia Island Archives, Fernandina Beach, Florida 1960.

Measuring Worth. 2006. Accessed 2020.

    <http://www:measuringworth.html>

Pirate Gold is Believe to Be Buried on Amelia Island is Lure for Treasure Hunters

    Cover, The Florida Times-Union, November 29, 1935.

Uillian, Lou, Personal conversation with Rex Stocker and Helen Uillian. 2020.

PHOTOS & ILLUSTRATIONS

APPRECIATION PAGE

Thanks to the *News-Leader* for allowing the author permission to use an article.

Thanks to the *Fernandina Chamber of Commerce* for allowing the author to use an unpublished letter.

Thanks to *The Florida Times-Union* for permission to use an article published in 1935.

Special thanks to William L. Taylor, for putting our group on the location on the South End (with permission).

Thanks to Helen Ullian and Rex Stocker for allowing the author to use Lou's map.

Thanks to Donna Cloyd (granddaughter), Travis Cloyd (great-grandson), and Carissa Cloyd (great-granddaughter), of T. Howard for allowing the author for a use of a photograph.

Printed in the United States
by Baker & Taylor Publisher Services